Victorian
VECTOR MOTIFS

> **GREEN EDITION**
>
> **At Dover Publications we're committed to producing books in an earth-friendly manner and to helping our customers make greener choices.**
>
> Manufacturing books in the United States ensures compliance with strict environmental laws and eliminates the need for international freight shipping, a major contributor to global air pollution. And printing on recycled paper helps minimize our consumption of trees, water and fossil fuels.
>
> The text of this book was printed on paper made with 10% post-consumer waste and the cover was printed on paper made with 10% post-consumer waste. At Dover, we use Environmental Defense's Paper Calculator to measure the benefits of these choices, including: the number of trees saved, gallons of water conserved, as well as air emissions and solid waste eliminated.
>
> Please visit the product page for *Victorian Vector Motifs* at www.doverpublications.com to see a detailed account of the environmental savings we've achieved over the life of this book.

By Alan Weller.
Designed by Jennifer Lanes

Copyright © 2011 by Dover Publications, Inc
Digital images copyright © 2011 by Dover Publications, Inc.
All rights reserved.

Victorian Vector Motifs is a new work, first published by Dover Publications, Inc., in 2011.

The illustrations contained in this book and CD-ROM belong to the Dover Vector Motifs Series. They are royalty-free, and may be used as a graphic resource provided no more than ten images are included in the same publication or project. The use of any of these images in book, electronic, or any other format for resale or distribution as royalty-free graphics is strictly prohibited.

For permission to use more than ten images, please contact:
Permissions Department
Dover Publications, Inc.
31 East 2nd Street
Mineola, NY 11501
rights@doverpublications.com

The CD-ROM file names correspond to the images in the book. All of the artwork stored on the CD-ROM can be imported directly into a wide range of design and word-processing programs on either Windows or Macintosh platforms. In order to take full advantage of the unique capabilities of the vector format images you will need a vector-editing program such as Adobe Illustrator or CorelDRAW. As a bonus, we have included the freeware vector editor Inkscape on this CD. For more information, see the Read Me! file in the Inkscape folder on the CD. For the most up-to-date information about using the image files on this CD, please visit www.doverpublications.com/p991423.

ISBN 10: 0-486-99142-3
ISBN 13: 978-0-486-99142-9

Manufactured in the United States by Courier Corporation
99142301
www.doverpublications.com

001

002

003

004

005

006

007

1

008

009

010

011

012

013

014

015

016

017

018

019

020

3

021

022

023

024

025

026

027

4

028

029

030

031

032

033

034

5

035

036

037

039

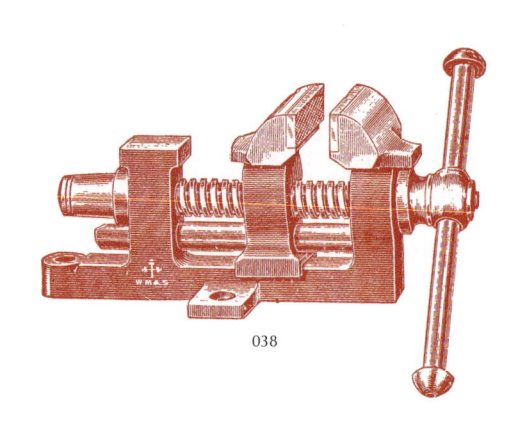

038

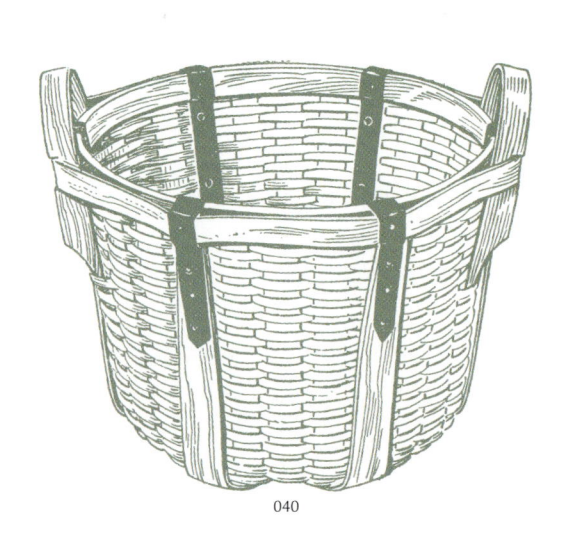

040

041

042

043

044

045

046

047

7

048

049

050

051

052

053

8

054

055

056

057

058

059

060

061
062
063
064
065
066
067

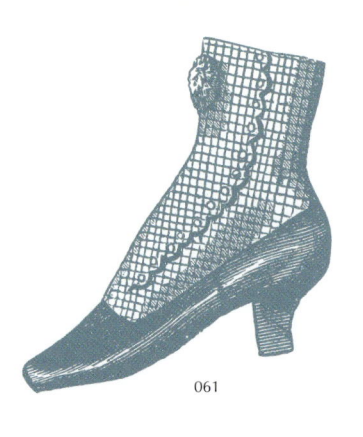

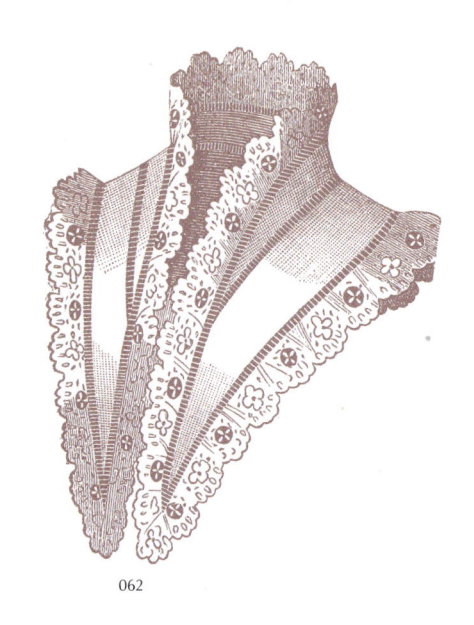

068

069

070

071

072

073

074

11

075

076

077

078

079

080

081

12

082

083

084

085

086

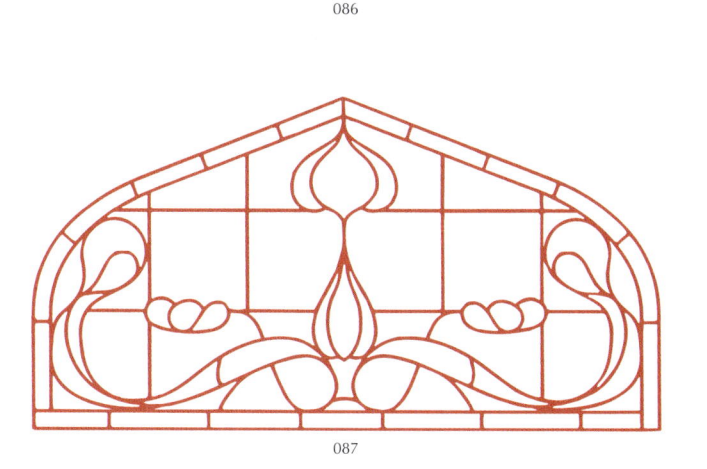

087

088

13

089

090

091

092

093

094

095

096

097

098

099

100

101

15

102
103
104
105
106
107
108

16

109

110

111

112

113

114

115

116

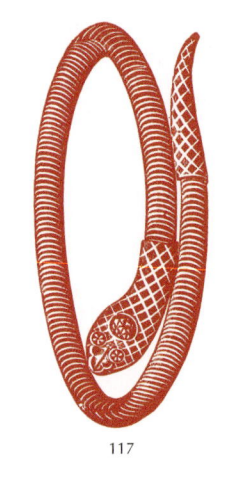

117

118

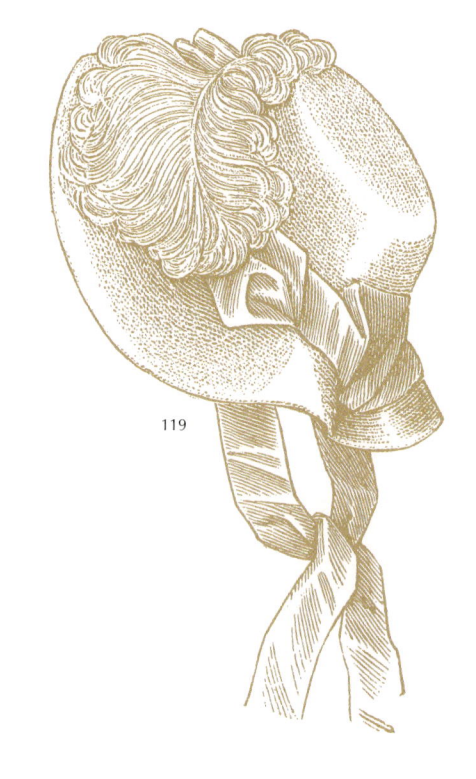

119

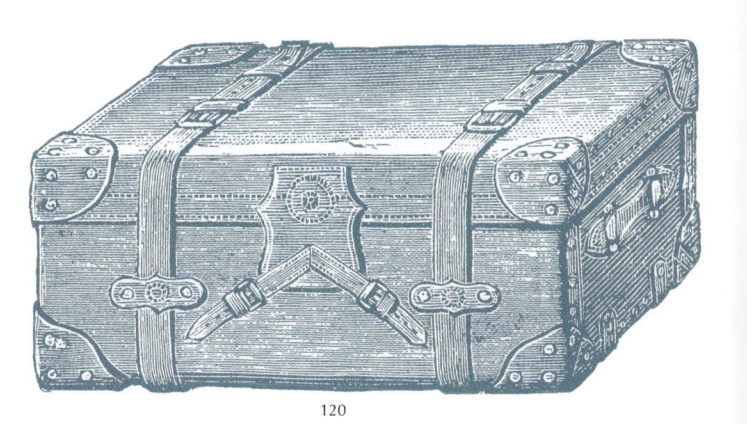

120

18

121

122

123

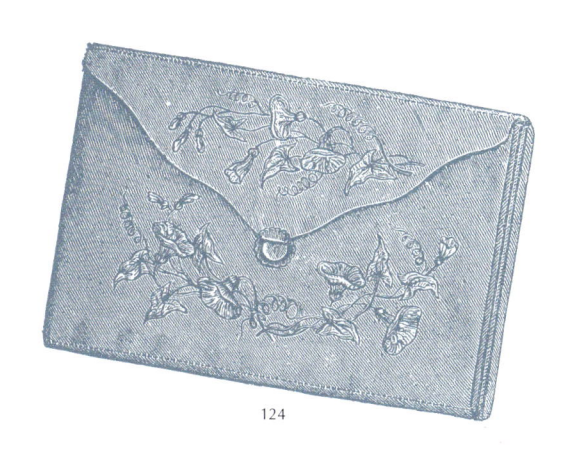

124

125

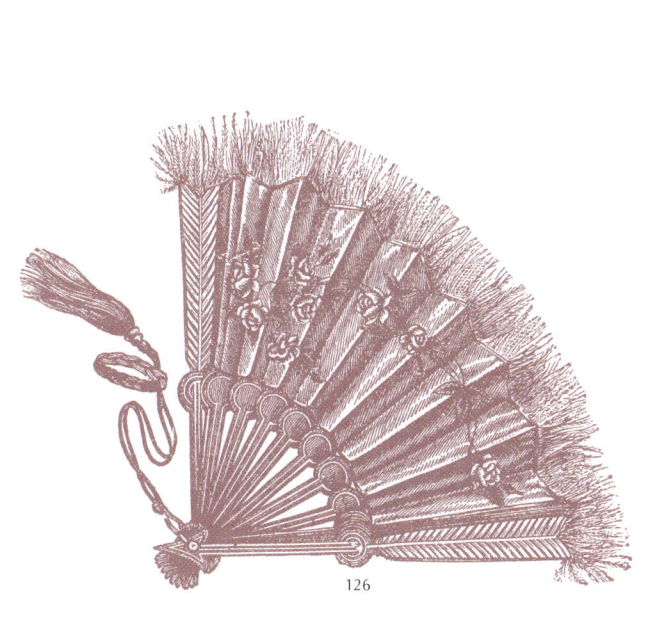

126

127

19

128

129

130

131

132

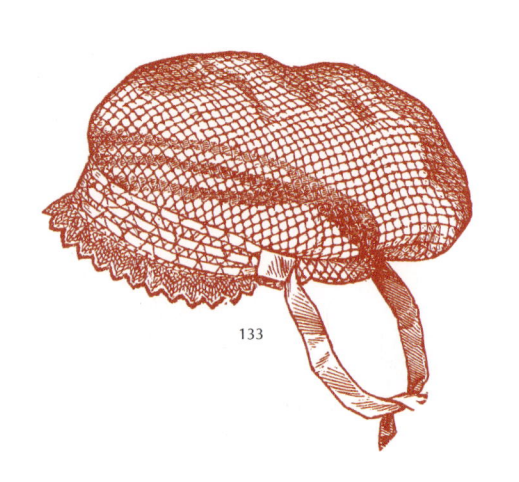

133

134

20

135

136

137

138

139

140

141

142

143

144

145

146

22

23

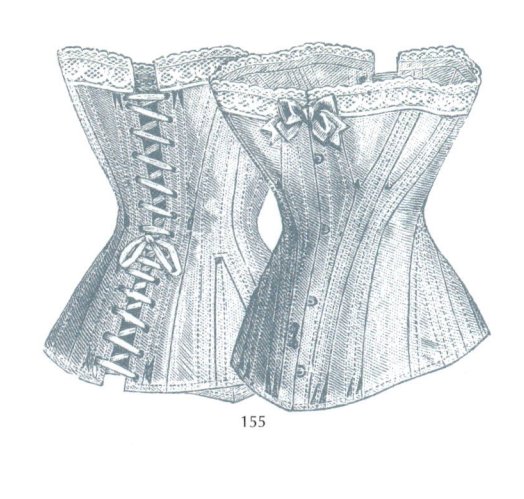

155

156

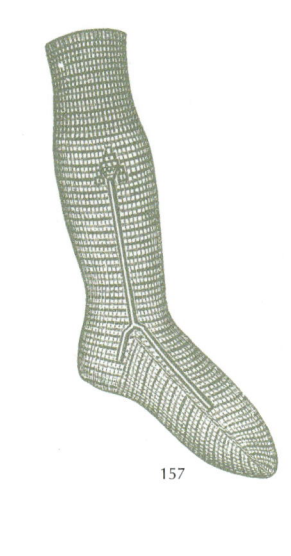

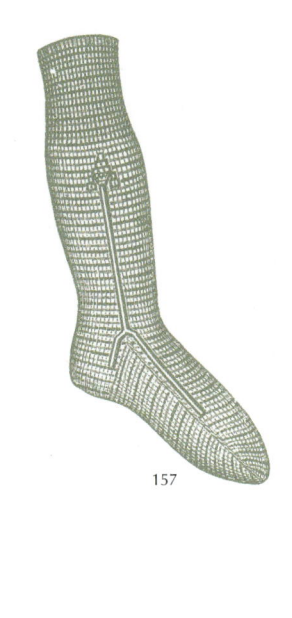

157

158

159

160

24

161

162

163

164

165

166

167

168

169

170

171

172

26

173

174

175

176

177

27

28

184

185

186

187

188

189

29

190

191

192

193

194

195

196

197

198

30

199

200

201

202

203

204

205

31

206

207

208

209

210

211

212

213

32

214

215

216

217

218 219 220

33

221

222

223

224

225

226

227

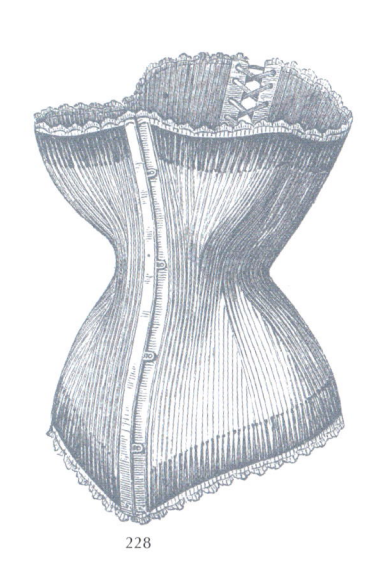

228

229

230

231

35

232

233

234

235

236

237

238

239

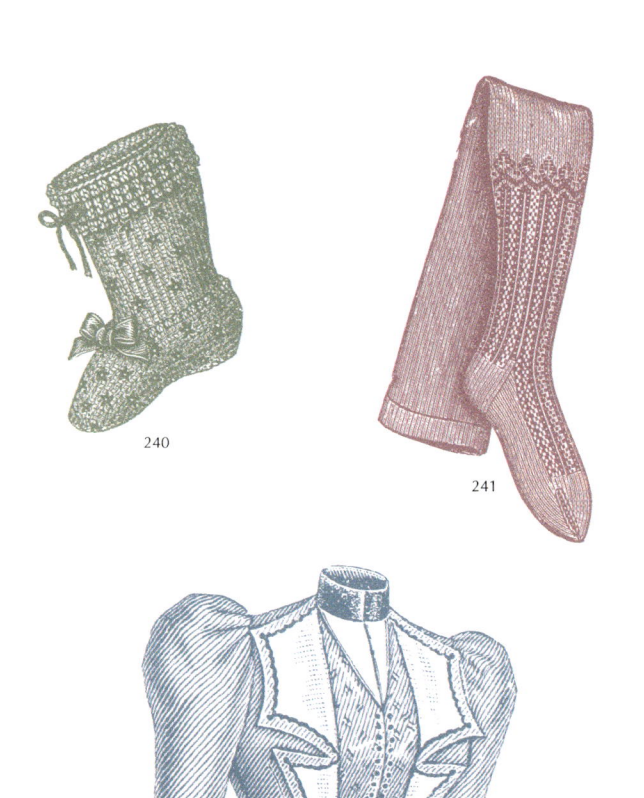

240

241

242

243

37

244

245

246

247

248

249

250

251

252

253

254

255

256

257

39

258

259

260

261

262

263

264

265

40

266

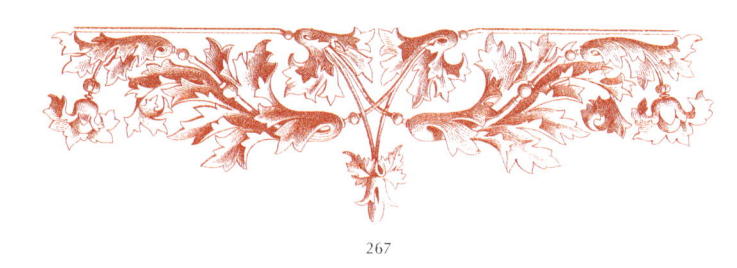

267

268

269

270

271

272

273

41

274

275

276

277

278

279

280

42

281

282

283

284

285

286

287

43

288

289

290

291

292

293

294

44

295

296

297

298

299

300

45